beneath the white lattice

Joel Savishinsky **Laura Boatner**
Lauren Muzek

with **Nicoletta M. Cosentino**

with **Alex Brown**

edited by **Amir Kapoor**

For permissions, bulk orders, or rights inquiries, contact:

Open Kimono Publishing, LLC

12740 York St, STE 64

Thornton, CO 80241

Info@openkimonopress.com

www.openkimonopublishing.com

Library of Congress Cataloging-in-Publication Data

Beneath the White Lattice featuring prize-winning poems by:

Joel Savishinsky, Laura Boatner, and Lauren Muzek ; with additional works by Nicoletta M. Cosentino and Alex Brown.

1. American poetry—21st century.

2. Poetry anthologies.

3. Open Kimono Publishing. I. Savishinsky, Joel. II. Boatner, Laura. III. Muzek, Lauren. IV. Cosentino, Nicoletta M. V. Brown, Alex.

Description: First edition.

Identifiers:

Hardcover ISBN: 978-1-961763-24-1

Paperback ISBN: 978-1-961763-23-4

E-book ISBN: 978-1-961763-25-8

Subjects: LCGFT: Poetry.

Classification: PS3602.R6965 A6 2025 | DDC: 811.6

Library of Congress Control Number: 2025945620

Library of Congress Control Number available at: https://lccn.loc.gov/
2025945620

Contributors

Primary Author:

Nicoletta M. Cosentino

Featuring Poetry by the Winners of the Open Kimono Publishing Inaugural 2024-2025 Poetry Competition:

• **First Place Winner: Joel Savishinsky—**

"The Letters Rise and Re-assemble Themselves"

• **Second Place Winner: Laura Boatner—**

"America's Precipice"

• **Third Place Winner: Lauren Muzek—**

"Summer Sky"

Each contributing poet retains the text copyright to their respective works, which appear in this collection with their permission.

Credits

Edited by Amir Kapoor

Designed by Amir Kapoor

Production Details

Printed in the United States of America

First edition, 2025

————————————

Cover and interior design managed by Open Kimono Publishing, with design by Amir Kapoor.

Bulk & Special Orders

Our books may be purchased in bulk for promotional, educational, or business use. For inquiries, please contact **Info@openkimonopress.com**.

Follow Open Kimono Publishing:

Website: www.openkimonopublishing.com

Facebook: www.facebook.com/openkimonopublishing

X (Twitter): www.x.com/openkimonopub

Instagram: www.instagram.com/openkimonopublishing

introduction

Life is a paradox. It offers us wonder and weight in equal measure—telling us we can be anything while quietly handing us limitations we never asked for. Still, I love this life. I love it because I know it—because I've seen both its beauty and its flaw—and still choose to believe in its possibility. Like all things worth loving, it is complicated.

This book is not a declaration. Nor is it an escape. It is an attempt to stand in the tension—to explore what it means to exist, to dream, and to carry hope inside a world that rarely makes sense.

The title, *Beneath the White Lattice*, is a metaphor for that world. For the unseen structures, the quiet patterns, the unspoken rules that shape our days. Beneath them, we make our way. We stumble. We endure. We find grace in fragments, and meaning in the spaces others pass by.

This collection is a chorus of voices—Joel Savishinsky, Laura Boatner, and Lauren Muzek, the prize-winning poets selected through Open Kimono Publishing's Inaugural 2024–2025 Poetry Competition—alongside Nicoletta M. Cosentino and myself. Each poem is a reflection, a reckoning, a reminder.

Some speak in quiet tenderness; others confront with unflinching force. But all of them, in their own way, are alive.

Together, they offer a mosaic of the human experience—not just the milestones, but the moments in between. The breath before a decision. The ache of longing. The stubborn joy that rises in the face of exhaustion. The ordinary beauty of being here at all.

The poems you'll find here weren't chosen because they agreed with me, but because they stirred something true. I believe the purpose of art is not to tell us what we already believe—but to help us see with sharper eyes and softer hearts.

You won't find conclusions here. You'll find contradictions, grace, and quiet truths. My hope is that something in these pages reaches you—reminds you that you are not alone in the questions you carry.

So take a breath.

Read slowly.

And ask yourself—not what this life is, but what it could become, if we allowed ourselves to live it more honestly.

—Alex Brown

one
the letters rise and re-assemble themselves

Joel Savishinsky

We know, in our tired bones and
wounded hearts that even small acts

help bring big dreams closer to fruition,
that through our own actions

we must compensate for those
who refuse to carry their portion

of the weight of history, those who
would rather wring their hands

than ring their neighbors' doorbells,
who shake their heads instead of

shaking the cornerstones of complacency,
resignation and sclerotic institutions.

Like the prophets of an earlier age,
we sense that our knowledge is

limited but our responsibility infinite.
We can see our task as either a burden

or a joy, and can embrace or reject it…
but cannot avoid the need to choose,

which in both the moment and in the end
is our condition and life's only real question.

On the final day, the letters of all the books
will rise from the pages and re-assemble

themselves into a new testament, which will
ring with terror and the terrible story
of our deeds.

two
america's
precipice

Laura Boatner

It starts with one stone
a chipping away, chiseling of sorts
digging to China as my mother always
said

In China it was pounded into sand
their people have known it
for seven decades or so

Here, babbling brooks, once slick as silk
have rough edges now etched
into fifty pieces, maybe fifty-one

A carnival barker yelling;
flushed face, eyebrows furrowed
the color of honeydew, or more
fluorescent than that

Stones and bricks in a road leading to Oz
because this doesn't feel quite real
and the curtains are pulled back

Judges, legislators,
one at a time acquiescing
out of fear, reprisal
is this really happening?

to us of all people?
right now?
like we're a scarecrow of sorts?

In one-hundred days
the rocks have become boulders
on shoulders of complacency

David threw a rock at Goliath
hitting the target
unlike we at the strongman

A mountain of stone
penetrated upon and fissured
and it's on this precipice that
we now stand

three
summer sky

Lauren Muzek

The sun is high

Spirits, higher

Blue skies

Long days

Chlorine drenched eyes

Clangorous youth

Untouched by age

Toes raw from bottomless fun

Days soaked in sun

Bathed in protection

Constant reflection

Lauren Muzek

Swaying side to side

Smiles, ear wide

poetry by

Nicoletta M. Cosentino

one
lost my voice

I lost my voice,
way back when I was three.
What I learned at that age
was the exorbitant fee.

I decided to trade,
my voice for
my peace.
It was quite deceptive
'cause I thought it was
on lease.

But it turns out
I had the need to renew
this lease.
My voice for my peace
over and over

Through the years
it became more costly,
my voice, you see—

sounded too softly.
No one could hear it
not even me.

So in a sensible move
because it was apparent,
my voice for my peace
was a necessary component
for my survival
I continued this lease.

And faced the fee
there was no discount.
It was fair market value,
peace was found...

Pending—

Losing me.

erasing myself

To enable myself
to survive—
I need those I love
to be well and alive.

I want what
you want
I'll easily
agree.
If anyone is unhappy
I won't let it
be—
because of me.

Please don't notice me
at all.
I'm trying so hard
to blend into the wall.

I cross out my name
in hopes that you

don't see—
the choices I've made,
how I ended up being me.

Erasing myself
a lifetime worth,
can't see—
won't see—
don't see—
invisible on earth.

Bit by bit,
piece by piece
anxiety mounts
'cause I don't count.

Leaving me lonely
and fully alarmed,
trying to fix
what I have harmed.

Unknowingly
attempting
to replace myself.
Good works for
shame.
A physical body
full of pain.

Too shy to ask
but desperate
for mercy.
Hoping someday
to be found

worthy.

Don't know when
I'll be able to
return—
first I have to
learn, learn learn.

three
afraid

PANIC stricken
nothing feels right.
Terrified.
Shaking.
Hands frozen.
Face hot—
nowhere is safe.
Squeezing the breath
out of me.
Pain.
What if
It won't go away?
Alarmed!
HELP!
SO SCARED!

four
a way out

Please stop.

Arguing shreds me into little pieces,
crumbled to the floor.

Yelling crushes my soul
shaking me like thunder.

My senses can't function
when those I love
don't get along.

Frantic searching
for nearest exit.
Have to get away
or I won't survive.

Needed desperately:
A way out.

listen instead

GOD'S Plan
is hard to see.
Ignore yourself ,
listen instead—
hear God's words.
His Will is your help,
strive to be attentive.
Know the difference between
yours and God's intention.

God's plan
will only reveal
with practice
and prayer.
To open your resolve—
listen instead.

Fight the inclination
to your own will.
Lean towards God—

Listen instead,
do his will.

Are you listening?

17

no more joy

No more joy.
My heart's broken.
Does it matter?
No one tries to fix anything
I keep trying—
It doesn't matter.
No difference,
I'm exhausted
so tired.
Head hurts,
stomach is
always on edge of roller coaster—
waiting to drop.
Breaking everything,
no one listens.
So broken and tired
WHY can't I fix anything?
Joy is non-existent.

best friend

I have a best friend,
her name is Routine.

Always consistent,
never changes
I can count on her!

Safe and protected,
secure and shielded.
If Routine is present—
I might make it
through each day.

Routine and I
work well together.
Don't mess with her
or I'll crumple.

She's the best
I'm very grateful.
Through her—

life can be
not so hateful.

Never unfriend me—
please,
Routine!

my heaven

GOD'S LOVE

A kaleidoscope of wildflowers,
upon rolling hills.
Short sprinkles,
of light rain.

GOD'S LOVE

Birds in symphony,
luminous sun,
buoyant breeze.

GOD'S LOVE

Trees of wine-cookies
ready for picking.
People I love
within hugging distance.

GOD'S LOVE

All doggies from my life
here to greet me,
tails wagging,
hearts full.

GOD'S LOVE

No anger,
hurts removed,
regrets disappear.
Sadness absent,
pain nonexistent.

GOD'S LOVE

Peace and safety
envelope me,
no anxiety,
no worries.
Contented in my Heaven.

nine
edge

One foot in
one foot out.
Teetering
on the edge
unable to do more.

Never the right move.
Never the right thing.
I can't fix it all.
I can't fix a thing.

One foot in
one foot out.
Trying so hard
hanging onto the edge—
but falling anyway.

I can't hurt much more—
my cracked heart won't heal.
Everyone is angry—
I don't want to feel.

One foot in
one foot out.
Weary with fatigue.
Exhaustion taking over.

Fingers are slipping
edge getting sharper.
I can't see the bottom,
nothing is helping.

No foothold left—
falling fast.
Hope is waning.
How do I last?

Lights dimming.

make-believe

In my make-believe dollhouse
the fuzzy animals wear cute clothes.
They all get along,
and no one cares
if you're different.

The lions frolic with the moo cows,
the bunnies romp with the tigers.
All is well in my dollhouse,
everything is tidy with space to have fun.

No one raises their voice,
we all just sing along.
We flush the pretend toilet
because the sound is a song.

You can use the stairs
but you're also welcome to hop
floor to floor.
You can play anywhere,
no reason to shut the door.

The beds are cozy and
the food is everlasting.
Windows stream sunlight
and safety is assumed.
Worries never even
enter your mind—
in my make-believe dollhouse.

Happiness abounds,
love is all around.
And you never have to mow
the grass
because nature
surrounds.

There's a truck
that everyone fits in—
and a horse
as big as The truck.
If you want the horse inside—
you're in luck.
'Cause everyone is welcome.

The only rule
is to be kind—
and if you feel
Like doing the chicken dance,
no one ever minds.

I am so content,
in my make-believe
dollhouse.
There's Even a giraffe
with bells on her skirt.

I bet her heart
never even hurts.

If you'd like to visit
or even stay for a while—
the lights are always on
and no one needs to cry.

farm memories

I can still feel the hot sun on my face. The smell of dusty, gritty dirt and fresh green growing asparagus fills my nose. My Grandpa dropped us off on the short dirt road after riding on the big tractor from the fields. My grandparents worked all morning hoeing the rows and rows of asparagus, while my sister and I ran and played in the field. My grandma leads us to the raised cement surrounding the well. My sister and I sit on the cool, rough cement while my grandma gets the cup she stores in a little box on the well and fills it with cold water from the well pump. We all share the cup and drink the icy cold water from the well. It tastes so fresh and quenches our thirst after being in the dusty field all morning. We rest for a moment under the shade of a big tree that shades the well and enjoy this little break in the day. Then my grandma wipes off the cup with her bandana, puts it back in its little box and says "Let's go make lunch.", and we all walk towards the house with thoughts of Italian bread sandwiches, fresh from the garden salad and a juicy watermelon for dessert. Summer days at my grandparents' farm were lovely.

it's killing me

Slowly
It's killing me
from the inside
out.
Starting with a crack
right
through my heart...

Filling my stomach
with ulcers of pain
'till I can't think straight
and wonder if I'm sane.

This can't be—
my mind says clearly,
through all this time
even yearly
we are all close,
love surrounds,

Now only

hostility
can be found.

How
can this happen?
How
can this be?
All the deadly anger
makes me
need
to flee.

My heart is no longer strong
it's worn out.
With no song
my stomach
bleeding
slowing feeding
this death.

That's killing me
from the inside
out.

Stop!
I shout.

But no one
hears me.
It's too late
for my fate
my heart can't keep
beating.

When no one is willing to fix
what's broken—
give benefit of doubt
instead of
hating
and reconciling
instead of fighting.

Is any of this important?
Can't anybody see
what all of this
is doing to me?

It's all my doing
they say
I am to blame.
I've let it all happen
So the pain is laid
at my feet.

And my heart won't beat.

It will stay broken
my stomach
will keep paining
my eyes will keep
raining.

Slowly—
it's killing me.

thirteen
an unfinished poem

A
Life
Remembrance

You were hurting too
at the time I met you.
Strong and grown up outside
a lost child inside.
We were both
a walking open sore—
unable to heal.
Time had stood still.
In your eyes I could see
the same hurt and unhappiness
so familiar to me.
Parting separately,
to live our lives as we knew—
we should find it
comforting to know
I wasn't alone.
Even if...

and that's how you became
an unfinished poem.

34

poetry by

Alex Brown

one
the price

We sell our souls for a taste.
Money lays all of us to waste.
It carves the hours from our thin skin,
a debt that grows but won't rescind.

The clocks don't tick;
their unforgiving hands gnaw and bite.
A steady feast—
on each of our damned days and nights.

We trade our lungs for bitter polluted air,
our hands for work for nothing, only despair.
Our bones are ground to line their streets,
While hunger pangs curl—
between filthy sheets.

Steal laundry detergent to be locked away.
For a dollar, they imprison us, our souls to
    stay.

Our cents cemented in pockets of the rich,

stowed tight.
Let us don a velvet noose in broad daylight.
We spend our youth, we spend our breath,
we buy our way literally into our death.

And still, they watch with dollar signs,
hollow empty eyes,
counting profits as we as a people die.

two
pareidolia

I got lost.
"You want to go that way,"
a voice from nowhere calls.
But the map is a ghost, the road a lie.

Why are we running?

To wash our hands of the cunning,
to scrub away fingerprints we never left.
Who did this? Who?
Another drink—
to rinse the stench
of something beyond decay,
the way the dead call, the way they decay.

Sails rise, wind howls,
tomorrow is an unlit shore.
We drift toward it anyway.

The voices repeat,
threading voices through the laces of my shoes.

Where is she? Is she okay?
You don't look so good.
And the street is nothing—
but a cobblestone throng.

Gasping for air,
scratching in disrepair,
slapping my own face—
wake up, wake up—
inhale fire, boil in its taste.
I open the door. She was here.
She said there was something wrong,
with this place.

It doesn't make sense.
What do we make
of the white-lacquered fence?
What day is it?
I'm having a great time.
No, I am not.
I am not.

I'm sorry, what is this?
What is that?

Crazy?

I knew it.
They crown us in raspberries and champagne,
watch as the bubbles rise in our throats.
To control is to rewrite.
To rewrite is to unhinge.
It is working.

Forgetting is a gift.
I pray to receive it.
But I see it—everywhere.
Even in the grain of wood,
the ghostly rings its petrified stained glass,
the face in the smoke.

Pareidolia in everything seen—
it's all that truly lasts.

three
enough

I don't want more, I just want enough.
Enough to live.
Enough to pursue a life.
One of freedom.
A pursuit of happiness.

Four numbers for the plunders.
There is no forgiveness.
Just forgetting.
Losing opportunities, submitting.

My hands shake, my voice hoarse.
I scream into a vat of silence,
trampled by my horse
To own anything - just an illusion.
These things own you, they are the contusion.

So I lance the lesion flowing to my heart.
I watch everything as my world falls apart.
One for all and all for nothing.
Out of many one, grinning, bluffing.

Alex Brown

I might have something for you.

A debt without a name,
a weight without form.
The cost of breath, the price of warmth.
Wages, rations - freedom's fraction.
The contract signed in absent action.

What is this dream but a borrowed sun,
a rented sky, a thought undone?
Each dawn, the lock clicks shut again,
golden handcuffs, paper-thin.

They taught us to kneel before the lie,
to bless the whip, to deify
the hunger that keeps the wheel in motion,
the drowning thirst we call devotion.

But enough was never ours to take.
It's promised, rationed,
stripped away by their rake.
A dangling fruit, a hollow fate,
a feast behind an empty guarded gate.

So tell me now, what must be done?
Shall I carve the sun out of the sky?
Shall I unchain the morning, burn the debt,
sharpen hunger into a cry?

For I have nothing left to give,
no more to bargain, no more to live
as a pawn inside this damned lie.
A body numbered, a soul unnamed.
I long for freedom,

but I subsist tamed.

I'm borrowing each second,
each breath I take.
This war of subservience-
It's more than I can fake.

I don't want more.

I just want enough.

four
wxkop23q

My order ID, WXKOP23.
My only chance at hope, a lottery.
I bought a ticket on money borrowed.
My only chance, a tomorrow followed.

The numbers print like prophecy,
black ink curling like fate's decree.
Not a birthright, not a plan -
just six digits to unmake a man.

WXKOP23Q -
a name more real than the one I knew.
A lifeline inked in barcode's binary breath,
a rope that pulls me back from death.

They say it's chance, they say it's luck.
But I know better - I'm stuck, I'm struck.
This is the way the world will end:
a slip of paper, a bet, a bend.

The house always wins, but I don't care.

I place my prayer in thinning air.
God of lotteries, fate's machine,
spit out mercy in fiat paper so obscene.

WXKOP23Q -
a coded wish, a numbered plea.
I'd sell my past, I'd sell my skin,
I'd carve these digits deep within.
I've nothing left - no cards to play.
No savings, no escape, no way.

The world is rigged, the game is cruel.
And yet, I scratch, I spin the spool.
The clerk hands me my slip with ease,
not knowing,
I am cut down teetering on my knees.

A quiet laugh, a nod, a sigh -
they do not know that if I die,
it's numbers drawn, or else all is nigh.

I check my ticket under the light.
Six numbers roll—
my heart throbs a thick tired hum.
One by one, the digits come.

8-13-19-20-31-34

WXKOP23Q -

My only chance, my final pour.
To win is to lose,
to lose is to live.
I'm shameful, desperate,

there's nothing I wouldn't give.
Bamboo shives driven up my fingernails.
This is my water, I carry it in pails.
So it goes, so it gives.

Will I win?

I know the answer,
a red x hastily painted on my door.
I watch helplessly sinking deep into the floor.
Who knows what we've been through,
who counts the final score?

This is it, morally bankrupt,
this war is a race - and there is no more.

five
every night

You know what's gonna happen right?
Chasing that dragon into the night?
Another day sorting through the squalor.
Feel your sanity shaving away, chiseled smaller.

Boxes of death stuffed in the closet.
Another failed deposit.
The pots still steaming.
I'm inside screaming.

Scratching, clawing.
I'm mauled, the consistent gnawing.
Teeth like debts sink into marrow,
Hollowed veins trace lines so narrow.

A spoon's reflection warps my face,
dissolving time, erasing my space.
Walls breathe in, a throat constricted,
The devil leers, my limbs afflicted.

Nails crack, stripped to the root,

a body reduced to blackened fruit.
Cough up ghosts, thick with tar,
Lost in a car crash burning from afar.

The door won't open, the lock is fate,
A pulse still knocking - but it's too late.
You know what's gonna happen right?
I do, it happens every night.

under the thumb of the south portico

I was born in a waiting room
and I've been waiting ever since—
for something to change
that was never mine,
it was always beyond my reach, that fence.
My mother bled in a hospital hallway
because they said she wasn't "in-network."
My father drank silence
because it was cheaper than therapy.
And I,
I learned to smile without feeling it
because the cameras are always on.

We live in the pause
between stimulus and permission.
We are the afterthought,
the footnote,
the meanwhile—
the slaughtered sheep of their ambition.
They hand us ballots like bandages
and tell us our voices matter

but count them only when convenient.
And still—
still we show up,
tattered and trembling,
holding out hope like it might get stamped,
like we're worth remembering;
and returned with interest.

It never is.
We are never remembered.
Our dreams are severed, grossly dismembered.

Behind the white columns
they eat steak from our arteries.
They drink wine aged in our sorrow.
They toast to the free market
as we auction our futures
for insulin,
for rent,
for another month of breathing
in a country that only loves us
when we're quiet.

Their suits are sewn with our overtime.
Their flights bought by our overdrafts.
Their vacations float
on oceans of our exhaustion.
And when they speak of the
"American people",
they do not mean us—
they mean the idea of us,
the myth of us,
the sanitized, sellable version
that never asks for too much

or speaks without raising a hand.

I have written letters,
marched until my feet forgot
how stillness felt,
called offices that sent me to voicemail
or nowhere at all.
And still,
I cannot afford the life I already live.

We are policed for breathing wrong.
We are blamed for drowning
in water they filled our lungs with.
We are told to pull ourselves up
with straps they cut
when we were children.
And when we scream,
they mute us with slogans—
Freedom.
Faith.
Family.
As if those words haven't been hollowed out
and sold back to us
with interest and fine print.

The South Portico looms
like a father who never said sorry.
It doesn't need to move—
its stillness is the threat.
A monument to decisions
we never got to make,
a palace built from the bones
of our bad options.

I am tired.
God, I am so tired.
Of smiling through trauma,
of celebrating crumbs,
of trying to outrun
the weight of a country
that kneels only for the flag,
never for its people.

But there is something
they cannot bury.
Something they forgot
when they traded souls for stock options.
It lives in the quiet rebellion
of teachers buying crayons—
with their own money.
In the janitor who hums a hymn
while scrubbing marble floors
he'll never walk in shoes that fit.
In the single mother
who turns canned beans into a feast
and still has the strength to dream.

It lives in me.
It lives in you.
And when the thumb presses hardest,
when it grinds down on our chests
and calls it order,
we will not flatten—
we will sharpen.
We will become the edge.
And they will remember
what it feels like
to live at our cliff's edge.

the american scheme

They called it a dream—
but we wake up in overdraft,
rent climbing like smoke
from a fire they pretend not to see.

Groceries ring up with guilt,
eggs priced like gold dust,
and the clerk doesn't look you in the eye—
he knows.
We all know.
We pay the price of their lust.

We weren't born poor,
we were priced into it.
Born beneath banners of freedom
we can't afford to wave.

We work
and we work
and we work
just to breathe in moldy apartments

with ceilings that leak
like promises from campaign mouths-
empty promises and nothing to seek.

They sit on silver hills, we listen to them speak;
their forks scraping filet,
talking wellness and hustle
while we boil tap water
and strain every muscle.

You're not lazy,
you're exhausted.
You're not failing,
you're being crushed—
on purpose.

Healthcare?
More like a game of roulette
where the house always wins
and your diagnosis
is an invoice, a fat litany paying for their sins.

They chant choice
but give us none.
Opportunity
but lock all the doors and run.
Justice
but only if your wallet can plead.

It was never a dream.
It was a scheme—
engineered in suits,
marketed with flags,
sold to you

with your own sweat.

Still, we wake up
and pour coffee we can't afford
into chipped mugs
with the word Hope
already faded,
the absurdity of being tied to a board.

We drink it anyway.

eight
the cost of
breathing

It begins
with the smallest grief:
an email unanswered,
a breath held too long in traffic,
a laugh that dies in your throat
before anyone hears it.
They watch us as they gloat.
We drown underneath, only our bodies float.

No one sees that we're drowning
in places water can't reach—
beneath fluorescent lights,
between calendar invites,
in the hush of 3 a.m.
when the world is asleep
and your thoughts are screaming.

They say just ask for help
but there's a cost to needing—
every confession of struggle
is a currency they count against you.

You're too much
until you're not enough.

They love survivors,
but only if you smile afterward.
Only if you turn your pain
into a commodity
or a startup
or a memoir
that ends with I made it.
No one claps for the ones
still in the fire.

You learn
how to look okay.
How to master
the sacred art of
the 15-minute cry
between meetings.
How to say "I'm good"
without choking
on the word.

But your soul knows better.
It catalogues the little deaths:
the dream you stopped naming,
the friend who stopped calling,
the room that feels like a punishment
instead of a home.

You stare at the mirror
like it owes you answers.
Like it might finally blink
and confess it's been lying—

that this isn't your face,
that this isn't your place.
Though this is our only life's taste.

You scream silently
into your morning residue,
bitter enough to burn,
but never strong enough
to wake you
from this life
you didn't choose.

You once believed
in the promise—
not heaven,
not fame,
just peace.
Just a day
where you didn't have to fight
your own mind
to make it out of bed.
Our hearts are muted, broken and tamed.

But the world sells anesthesia
disguised as inspiration.
Quotes in cursive on throw pillows.
Photos of beaches
you'll never walk on.
Advice from people
who have never known
the ache of an empty fridge
or the shame of borrowing joy
just to get through the day.

This isn't a cry for help.
This is our truth, the truth of the invisible.
For the ones who show up
when it hurts.
For the ones who raise children
and still cry on the floor.
For the ones who call it a win
just to be here.

You don't need to rise.
You don't need to shine.
Some days,
survival is the miracle.

And if no one told you today—
I see you.
Not the face you wear,
but the you
beneath your skin, the pain you wear,
the cracked vase
still carrying water,
the poem
still being written
even if your hands shake
as you are an extension of the ink's fodder.

Let it shake.
Let it spill.
Let it hurt.
Let it be real.

You're allowed
to live a life
that isn't pretty

but still means
everything.
The cost of breathing.
A failed test.
Our livelihoods were predetermined
by the vests.

i buried it beneath the floor

I buried it beneath the floor—
my sanity.
Laid it flat
like a rug that curled at the corners,
tucked it under the hollow boards
where no one would notice the splinters
or the whispering cords.

It was making too much noise.
Kept telling me things I didn't want to hear.
Kept crying
at inopportune moments—
at the grocery store,
at stoplights,
in line at the DMV.

So I folded it
like an apology letter I'd never send,
and nailed it down
with laughter
and to-do lists

and medication
I can't pronounce.

It didn't go quietly.
It thrashed.
It screamed.
It begged for one more chance to speak
without being edited.

But what was I supposed to do?
Let it live in the open?
Let it wander through staff meetings
and birthday parties
with its ribs exposed
and its eyes wild?

No.
I did what we all do.
I hid it.
I smiled.
I gave it a eulogy
only I could hear:
You were too much.
You made them uncomfortable.
You didn't fit in the shared drive or in my
    head.
You spoke in sobs when the world demanded
    the living undead.

Still—
on some nights,
when the house is too quiet
and the wine doesn't work,
I hear it scratching.

Not loud.
Just enough.
Like it's tracing the outline
of the life I was supposed to have
with its broken fingernails.

Each scratch
is a memory
I swore I'd rewritten.
The argument I laughed off.
The bruises I intellectualized.
The morning I stared into the mirror
and mouthed,
I don't want to do this anymore.

It's all still there,
under the floor.
Pulsing.
Waiting.

I walk across it every day.
Vacuum.
Sweep.
Watch the tea bleed out, a deep steep.
But it beats,
God, it beats—
not like a heart
but like a verdict.

And no one else hears it.
They say,
"You're doing so well."
"You look amazing."
"You're an inspiration."

But the floor knows.
It creaks beneath compliments.
It moans under productivity.
It remembers everything
I pretend I've forgotten.

And some days,
I kneel.
I press my ear
to the floorboards.
I listen.

And I swear
I almost answer.

out of office

They shut it down and walked away,
another stunt, another day.
A power game behind closed doors—
while hunger lines replace the stores.

They called it fiscal discipline,
but left us cold and locked within.
No checks, no aid, no heat, no light,
just empty fridges every night.

The parks are closed, the phones don't ring,
the vets get told to wait for spring.
The bills come due, but not the pay—
a silent war in broad midday.

They sit on leather, sip their scotch,
and smile while their donors watch.
But janitors and TSA
still show up broke receiving no pay.

They say we're strong, they say we'll cope,

but strength is not a substitute for hope.
And speeches don't repair the rent
When every dime we had is spent.

The suits get raises, perks, and flair—
while single mothers strip despair.
The paycheck's gone, the pantry bare,
but patriotism fills the air.

They wrap themselves in flags and prayers,
and swear they've answered all our cares.
Yet leave us waiting in the dark
for men who play with national sparks.

No justice here, no fair redress,
just endless talk and blame, no less.
They shut it down without a plan—
and called it brave to starve a man.
Their one job left undone,
it was according to their plan.

the liar

I am the liar.
Not by choice, or desire but by design—
fashioned in silence, walking the line
in rooms where truth is too ugly to abide
and fake smiles roll in and out like a tide.

I tell them I'm fine.
I nod in the right place.
My hands don't tremble
when I say, What a blessing,
though my soul's been erased.

This is the fire—
the one no one sees.
It's not flames or smoke,
just the tightening grip squeezing out hope.
I appear to be who they want me to be.

I wear the right clothes.
I laugh at the jokes.
I nod at the men

with wolf-thick throats
who shake hands like rope.

I perspire beneath it—
this skin of applause,
this fraudulence tailored
to keep me employed,
to survive their laws.

Don't call me brave.
Don't call me strong.
You haven't heard the prayer
I cry before
I pretend all day long, drowning in disrepair.

You haven't seen me peel off my smile
like a bandage at night,
or rock in the dark
because I said yes sir
when I wanted to fight.

I am the fake man.
The liar.
The one who curtsies to power
while choking on wire.

This isn't living—
this is sanctioned decay.
But I wear the lie
like an overgrown snake of a necktie
because truth doesn't pay.
It's not okay to be different,
To feel the emptiness; it requires a different
     display.

What choice do I have
when the truth makes them flinch?
When honesty costs
more than rent
and bleeds inch by inch?

So I lie.
I perform.
I make it look neat.
But inside, I'm burning
from head down to feet.

And one day—
if I vanish,
if I fail to appear—
just know I was honest
for one final year.

Until then,
I'll keep lying
to stay in this game.
I'll nod, I'll perform,
and forget my own name.

Because this is the price
for surviving their fire:
To be less than myself,
to be what cowards admire,
To be the fake man—
the liar.

twelve
lunarslave

I rise in the hush before gravity groans,
with bile in my throat and a buzz in my bones.
The engine is coughing, the silence is tight—
the world still asleep,
but I drive through the night.

The moon is my witness,
cold-blooded and pale,
she stares through the windshield,
detached from my wail.
Each turn of the wheel is a prayer in reverse—
I'm sick in the gut, rehearsing this curse.

The coffee is bitter, the thoughts are obscene,
I swallow my doubt like it's an antihistamine.
No one should rise when the stars still confess,
but I'm punching a clock in my funeral dress.

The road never ends, just loops on repeat,
with graves for the living beneath every street.
I drift to the job like a ghost through a wall—

half-man, half-memory, no self left at all.

I work underground in a hive with no queen,
a cocoon full of noise where we rot to stay
    clean.
Fluorescents above us like surgical light,
they bleach out the day and erase what feels
    right.

We speak in code, we barter in sighs,
trading whole lifetimes for prepackaged lies.
And no one looks up, and no one looks in—
we smile like we're paid just to bury the sin.

By seven, I emerge like a moth too late,
the sun disappeared, sealing my fate.
I drive home, half-mad, half-numb—
the night's only gift is the beat of a drum.

I am the vampire, cursed and confined,
a hunter of hours in a system designed
to drain us, to tame us, to call it success—
while daylight escapes through the tears in my
    chest.

I chase a currency I'll never own,
a dream built on debt, and a God made of
    stone.
They told me to strive, to grind and to run,
but I've only grown tired, and pale, and
    undone.

I give up. They have won.
They broke me with grace—

I smiled as I vanished,
erased my own face.

Let them count it as progress.
Let them call it a win.
But I've seen what they worship,
and I won't kneel again.

eyes like error codes

I.
They told me you're gifted,
then bolted me down—
chained to a glow
that replaced the whole town.

The hum grew into tinnitus,
and now my only sound.
It just itches, my eyes, my dying dry skin
a phantom, a thirst, a cognitive sin.

Blue light like cyanide bleeds through the air—
My pupils collapsing,
my spine glued to the chair.
I haven't stood up in at least seven years;
my reflection's a rumor
I dodge out of fear.

II.
They call it a job.

I call it decay.
Each keystroke another small flicker away
from whoever I was before backlit control—
my hands typed a future
that swallowed me whole.

The clever were cursed
to be fuel for the stream,
to drown in the data
they once used to dream.
And now I'm forbidden to matter or grieve—
just smile in emojis
then log out and leave.

III.
It started so slow—
just a twitch in the eye,
a blink that would stutter,
a screen that would sigh.
But then came the heat
like a wire through bone,
the buzzing of thoughts
in a language unknown.

I tried to look away.
God knows I tried.
But my salary
blinked in the margins,
and lied.
They warned me of burnout,
but never the smoke—
how vision combusts
when the human is broke.

IV.
My lashes are brittle, my sockets a mine,
mined for my effort
on company time.
Each hour's a hammer,
each deadline a drill,
my eyeballs now marbles
too tired to feel.

I scratched at the lids
just to see something real—
my own blood the color
of permanent teal.
The cursor kept blinking,
the inbox grew fat,
and sanity spat:
It's over. That's that.

V.
I tore at my hair like a wolf in a trap.
No air in the room,
just a fluorescent nap.
The code mocks my breathing,
the files grow tall,
I'm the ghost in the spreadsheet,
the ink on the wall.

I once wrote in language that could eat,
cajole, that bled—
now I write in compliance
with what must be said.
The poetry's gone,
replaced by commands—
Control-C, Control-V,

and my blood on my hands.

VI.
Now I sit,
half-blind,
fully aware,
that I've died into pixels
while still in this chair.
My heart is a widget,
my soul's just a graph,
my laugh auto-filled
with a canned paragraph.

My eyes—they fell out
while nobody watched.
They bounced on the desk,
then rolled toward the clock.
And still I kept typing,
because that's what we do—
we give them our bodies
and they bill us the rest.

VII.
So if you should ask why
my face looks so hollow,
why my voice is a 404,
hard to follow—
just know there was once
a boy built to write,
until they fed him poison
to the backlit night.

And if you should see him—
don't call him a name.

Alex Brown

Just hand him a mirror,
then walk away lame.
He'll try not to scream,
he'll try not to beg,
as he stares at his sockets
and a chair with one leg.

fourteen
the last place i looked

Happiness walks like someone I used to know.
I think we sat beside each other once
on a train I didn't want to board—
her mouth full of reasons to stay.
She never said goodbye,
just got off when I decided to stay.

Some days, I pretend I remember her laugh.
Other days, I can't even picture her face.
What I recall instead
is the numbness of not-feeling,
the silence that hums in-between,
like a house that's been abandoned
but still pays its own rent.

I've tried everything they said would work:
morning routines,
breathing exercises,
the kind of love you barter for in halves.
But the numbness is forever.
It rearranges the furniture of my brain

until even pain feels like wallpaper.

I don't want to be "happy".
I want a second—
just one—
where I forget what I'm carrying.
Lose everything I've done.
No matter the brevity, I crave such
A blissful escape.
A wincing moment of sleep,
without it all hovering above my face.
To forget my name,
my very existence, to be plain.

If happiness is real,
then it's the name of a ghost
and she no longer remains.
She's too tired to haunt me anymore.
But I still light a candle at night.
I stare at the flame, wondering
if it's her making it flicker.
I still leave the window cracked,
still practice the posture of hope,
though everything in me has dulled to a flesh
     pulp.
I'd trade my voice, my breath, my name—
for one moment where she returns,
unafraid,
and lets me forget
that I ever went looking.

The last place I looked—
she was gone, maybe because
she never was.

Alex Brown

I don't know her name,
Just the familiar game of the lust.
To feel something—how unfamiliar.
Happiness walks like someone I used to know.
She was a lie—it was all a show.

fifteen
i am the door

Everything is impossible—until it's not.
Nothing can be done, until it is.
Insanity scratches at itself until it's sane.
Doubt sleeps in every hallway, waiting.
It sharpens its teeth on your breath
and tells you: stop before you begin.

They said the sky would never open for you.
That maps were fixed.
That gravity had rules.
That names like yours don't make it past the
	gate.
They spoke in fences.
Built blueprints from their own fears
and dared to call it truth.

But truth is a fluid thing—
it spills when no one's looking.
Leaks beneath locked doors.
It gathers in your hands
when you have nothing left to hold.

I have stood in places
that were never meant to hold me.
Choked on the silence
until it croaked back in my voice.
I've felt the rules warp under my steps.
Watched the stone they swore couldn't crack
split clean in the middle
just because I stayed.

They forget:
the world doesn't ask for permission to
     change.
It just does.

Everything is impossible—until it bends.
Until the weight becomes momentum.
Until the "no" turns to noise,
and the noise turns to wind,
and the wind lifts your name
like it always belonged there.

I've seen the edge.
Tasted the nothing.
And walked anyway.

So let them say what can't be done.
Let them name the walls.
I am the door.